T0137508

HAIKU PUNishment

BOOK FOUR

Paul Treatman

iUniverse, Inc.
New York   Bloomington

Haiku PUNishment

Book Four

iUniverse books may be ordered through booksellers or by contacting:

iUniverse
1663 Liberty Drive
Bloomington, IN 47403
www.iuniverse.com
1-800-Authors (1-800-288-4677)

ISBN: 978-1-4401-2993-3 (pbk)
ISBN: 978-1-4401-3336-7 (ebk)

Printed in the United States of America

iUniverse rev. date: 3/25/2009

Acknowledgements

Thank you, Sylvia Rubin, your love and
devotion are my *raison d'être.*

This little volume is my latest in a quadrilogy (is this a word?) of
four books of haikus with a twist, the twist being the embedding of
a pun in the haiku context. HAIKU PUNishment follows HAIKUS
FOR PUNSTERS (book one),MORE HAIKUS FOR PUNSTERS
(book two) and A HAIKU/PUN FOR EVERYONE (book three).

My thanks for suggested pun offerings go to Sylvia Rubin, Bernie
Gutstadt, Dan Mann, John Thompson and Linda Lemay. In a
sense, they have paid me back for tolerating what I have inflicted
upon them though the years.

Dedication

To Abbe Jo and Jeffrey, Scott and Linda, Melissa and Bryon, Jennifer and Anthony and all their progeny, extant and future.

AND

To the cherished memory of
Elaine Treatman, who started it all.

FOREWORD

The haiku is a very old Japanese verse form that attempts to express cogently a thought in an economical three lines of 5 syllables, 7 syllables and five syllables. The haiku form was flowered in recent decades among poets as well as school children nationwide.

In this book, as well as in my previous three, I have melded the haiju form with the pun – a form of humor considered lowly by many. Not I. I have always loved and used puns, especially when I wanted to get thrown out of parties that bored me.

Puns have been used by poets, including Shakespeare, even before the haiku appeared. The pun is a word or expression that is a play on words. The pun might be a word with a double meaning within the context of the thought expressed. It might be a word that by design almost sounds like another word different from the word that the listener or reader might have expected. It might be a two-word expression whose first letters have been deliberately transposed for a hopefully comic effect. Mrs. Malaprop's mindless malapropisms were also puns.

All of these haikus are mine. Most of the embedded puns are mine. A few puns I did appropriate from the general domain and the chatter from cyberspace. I wove the puns into the haikus, a literary marriage that I pray will entertain you.

Feel free to use the puns in any context that makes sense or nonsense to you.

Paul Treatman

She: "Your fingers are
All over me!" He: "Because
I've gone digital."

Cartoonist frequents
A shooting gallery, learns
To be a quick draw.

Mrs. Malaprop:
"Look at such a handsome groom
With that sour bridle!"

"Did your girl friend teach
You that card game?" "No, not yet,
But I canasta."

"Cotton farmer prays:
"Deliver me from weevil,"
As he calms with psalm.

Pathologist starts
To sneeze in her lab, quickly
Gropes for her tissues.

My rule of eating
Three meals a day is simply
Alimentary.

Boy loses his pooch,
Searches far and wide, end quest
With a loud "Doggone!"

In some states, rooster
Fights are condemned by the law
As crime of fowl play.

A scantily dressed
Woman refuses to put
On her petty coat.

Convicted landlord
Decides to reform and turn
Over a new lease.

British sea captain
Hunting in the seven seas
As the Prince of Whales.

Stolen vehicles
Often end up in chop shops
For autotopsies.

So anxious to write
This new haiku book that I
Hit the ground punning.

My left shoe falls in
Love with my right shoe because
The pair are sole mates.

An anxious "Dear John"
Sleeps fitfully, expecting
Girlfriend's break-up call.

The eggs served at our
Breakfast are from happy chicks
And they were just laid.

Old man and his wife
Get knees replaced at same time.
A new joint venture?

Watching the gourmand
Eat could easily become
A gut-retching experience.

Psychiatrist says
He urges confused patients
To use mental floss.

Country dancing kids
Embark professionally
As the Polka Tots.

Innocent convict
Proclaims candidacy for
The Hall of Frame-up.

Gambler cries that he
Blew his salary in Lost
Wages, Nevada.

**Shopped in United
Arab Emirates? Well, then,
Dubai anything?**

Dallas merchant man
Heard singing sadly: Deep In
The Heart of Taxes.

A still-life painting
Of table settings, said critics,
Was pitcher perfect.

Dieter works out
On gym equipment –
Weapons of mass reduction.

Canine adopted
From animal shelter wins
A new leash on life.

Eve bit into the
Apple in what she called the
Garden of Eatin'.

Manufacturer
Of ovens does well as a
Man of convection.

In concert hall, son
And dad harmonizing on
Pianos Bach to Bach.

Degas cleverly
Painted from pigments of his
Imagination.

Autophile takes care
Of his collection of cars
With blood, sweat and gears.

A sad outcome of
This global warming can be
An emergent sea.

Our kids danced great in
Ballerina recital,
Looking tutu divine.

Husband praises wife
Who weaves own clothes, calling her
A perl of a girl.

Macbeth and wife plan
To kill king and rule, hope to
Sing, "Send in the Crowns."

Twelve little people
Hold a wild orgy, call this
Their own sex-couplets.

Sisters with implants
Strut proudly down city streets
As bosom buddies.

Female chess champ wants
Joint bank account; hubby asks:
"Who wants a checkmate?"

"Did the play have a
Believable plot?" "I found
It applausible."

Guests take umbrellas,
Cash, to get soaked or not at
The bridal shower.

Great artist invites
Newest love to his home with:
"Come see my itchings."

We grow too much and
Eat like horses. Consumption
Be done about this?

Husband: "Need to buy
Larger pants for the dance." Wife:
"Make Believe Ballroom?"

Motion picture star
Plays rich investment guru,
Enjoys his bank role.

Happy tourist in
Southern France finds the ladies
There oh, so Toulouse.

Israeli trenchermen:
"Arabs have all the oil, but
We get all the gas."

Sinful and guilty,
Decides to purge it all with
Milk of Amnesia.

Russian diplomat
Banished to Siberia –
Many a steppe down.

The divorce fight in
The courtroom was all about
The acrimoney.

Astronaut plans a
Visit to his mother, calls
It his Mission to Ma's.

Shawnee boat captain
Decides to wire a head for
A reservation.

Radiator firm
Posts a sign on side of truck:
We can fix your leak.

Probation: Scheming
Ex-con says: Call me on land
Phone or try my cell.

**Amtrak conductor
Says he is satisfied with
His station in life.**

Minister concludes
Nuptials with "I now pronounce
You husband and strife."

Famous author loves
Fishing, wants to change his name:
Ernest Herringway.

Writes book about her
Mom as a screaming shrew, "I
Dismember Mama."

The wedding cake is
Skyscraper tall; bride, groom feel
Like shedding some tiers.

A podiatrist
Into French cooking wants to
Create bunion soup.

Old English stories
With animal characters:
Canterbury Tails?

Oral surgeons ask:
Should dental x-ray films be
Considered tooth pics?

Dead drunk, he enters
Funeral home and shouts out
Loud: "I Want a Bier."

**When Julius sees his
Cleopatra, he starts to
Caesar and squeeze 'er.**

Old geezers reject
Foreign travel, prefer to
Stay in continent.

Are you so lovesick?
Yes, she is still the object
Of my affliction.

Podiatrist posts
New sign on his office door,
Reads "Time wounds all heels."

Poets plan wedding,
Review invitation list
For vetter or verse.

Couple speeds up the
Construction of home, hoping for
Imminent domain.

United Nations
Members acquire, exchange views
Using world of mouth.

Disgusted with his
Helpers, mechanic complains
Of his nuts and dolts.

Sign at restaurant:
Seven days without pizza
Surely makes one weak.

Men watching hula
Dancers swaying to music
Become hipnotized.

**Dairy industry
Publication run by an
Editor-in-cheese.**

**Back pain specialist
Posts sign on office door, "This
Is a lumbar yard."**

Gambler lays a buck
On a doe as he exclaims:
That's some faun, eh kid?

Internet expert
Teaches everything to son –
Chip off the old blog.

Chinese kids play Hide
And Seek, but they notice
The "it" boy is Peking.

Spy passing secrets
To the enemy is judged
A perpetraitor.

Keep browsing up and
Down the aisles, and know you're in
A stupormarket.

Optician says he
Was arrested once for fraud,
But claims he was framed.

Fainting at airport,
Tourist prays he does not have
Terminal illness.

Enjoy life, says doc,
Just swallow one milligram
Of frolic acid.

Customer finds shoe
Store empty, fuming there was
Not a sole in sight.

An interior
Desecrator furnished our
Brand new synagogue.

TV execs meet
On fishing trawler, agree on
Changing the network.

Curator in the
Museum spends loads on art,
Goes for baroque.

Sol, Rose get married
Christmas day, sing "Deck the Halls
With Vows of Solly."

Girl scolds her butcher
Boy friend because he once gave
Her the cold shoulder.

Madam to client:
"It was my business to
Do pleasure with you."

Tight economic
Times, tycoon decides to put
His grand yacht on sail.

Kids in bakery
Hold food fight. They all come through
With flying crullers.

Belgian greengrocer
Refers to his growing kids
As his brussels sprouts.

**Harvest time, farmer
Asks, "Are you an Idaho?"
"I yam what I yam."**

Uncertain Hamlet
Strolls courtyard and wonders, "To
Pee or not to pee."

They referred to my
Wife and me as fairy tale's
Beauty and the Least.

Confused traveler
To curvy airport clerk: "Two
Pickets to Tittsburgh."

Newspaper writer:
The George Bush Reign of Error
Finally over.

I was screaming, she
Complained, when the nurse gave me
An interjection.

Why did the crab cross
The ocean? Of course, to get
To the other tide.

He considered the
Scamming of his boss as the
Best crime of his life.

Mother makes jelly
With one man or another,
Marmalade many.

Dazzled by her looks,
He feels his heart filling with
Uncommon rupture.

Obama delayed
His V. P. choice, feeling he
Was Biden his time.

Goliath's mother
To son: "Avoid kid David,
You might end up stoned."

**Dorothy leaves farm
In winter and sings: "I'm Off
To See the Blizzard."**

In or out of the
Pool, she enjoys her coach's
Focus on breast stroke.

Pays a bundle for
Surgery, calls his O.R.
A classy clip joint.

Virgin bride, virgin
Groom off on a honeymoon
To be newlybeds.

Restaurant patron
Delights to find diamond
Ring in carat cake.

Rowdy customer
Storms out of car dealership
Of his own Accord.

Georgia teenagers
Cruise into town thought as the
Best for Macon out.

He ate so quickly
That he damaged his lip with
A fork just in tine.

Purported expert
Meat chef turning out to be
A flesh in the pan.

"Arsenic and Old
Lace" sisters buy cameras,
Still pixilated.

Mathematician
Calls wife's pubic area
Acute triangle.

Antiques dealer
Posts sign in front of store:
The Wizard of Odds.

Female soldier breaks Army regulations, gets Vaginal discharge.

Composer blends two
Genres of music, calling
It new Rock and Soul.

**Was our President
Really an incarnation
Of the Lyin' King?**

Movie directors show
Films in festival, where some
Cannes and some cannot.

Two gay Italian
Men speak lovingly about
Their innudendos.

Teen-age girls at the
Concert were screaming as though
Bit by some beetles.

Two-man argument
Includes invective with some
Cursory insults.

Yankee soldier breaks
Into Richmond church, looks to
Grab a Southern bell.

Dopey says he wants
To learn how to attach wheels
To miscarriages.

Travel to England
In the summer and get a
Taste of London Broil.

**New Delhi youngsters
Decide to develop own
Game of Hide and Sikh.**

From the frying pan,
Pardoned con goes monastic
Into the friar.

High glucose reading,
Patient seeks dialectic
Restaurant dishes.

Disgruntled Woman
Sheds her demanding husband,
Escaping bedlock.

Unfaithful husband
Learns new tricks with girlfriend at
A work semenar.

Roller rink prices
So very high it is no
Place for a cheapskate.

Trigonometry
Teacher conducts her classes
In a sine language.

Moses descends from
Mountain with headache, holding
Only one tablet.

Some say atheism
Is oft viewed as a non-prophet
Organization.

Some contrarian
Wall Street traders say they can't
Bear the bull market.

Trembling patient fears
Facial operation by
A spastic surgeon.

A vintner builds a
New winery to augment
His liquid assets.

Mom buys galoshes
For kids, raiding what she calls
Rainy day slosh fund.

Recidivist thug
Trailing a nun and wanting
To kick the habit.

Farm vet treats
Horse and soon returns it to
Stable condition.

Plagiarist faulted
When he chose to copy wrong
And not copyright.

**Indian tribe tries
To look young by bathing in
The fountain of Ute.**

She fell in love with
Her new caterer because
She loved his meatballs.

Polar bear caught on
Slab of ice – nowhere to go
But go with the floe.

A Lower East Side
Bagel store sign reads:
"From Schmear to Attorney Street."

Get the mammogram
Already, finally make
A clean breast of it.

Pennsylvanians dance
Polka at Christmas time, sing:
"Roll Out the Carol."

Chinese physicians
Treat a few spinal ailments
With backupuncture.

Ball players eat out
In restaurants but prefer
Running to home plates.

Frustrated seamstress
Advises daughter: As you
Sew, so shall you rip.

Sushi lovers in
Tokyo say they always love
Something to Nippon.

**Trader lamenting
In song: There's No Business
Like Slow Business.**

**Top fashion model
Wants to write her memoirs: "Days
Of Wine and Poses."**

**Steinbrenner begins
His memoirs of the Yankees:
"Once Upon a Team."**

Pirate admires his
Ill-gotten gains and exclaims:
It's so bootyful!

Floridian moves
West in order to find a
Warm Aridzona.

Gambler at racetrack
Hopes to see his win-dough of
Opportunity.

Smile, giggle or groan,
May my readers all enjoy
Haiku punmanship.

A female chemist,
Trying for pregnancy, keeps
Periodic charts.

Healing purple pill
Keeps your acid reflux from
The sarcophagus.

Schlimozal defined:
A victim of jerkumstance
Caused by a schlemiel.

A good allergy pill,
My doctor advises me,
Is nothing to sneeze at.

Athletic field crew
Demands steep salary boost
As great goal diggers.

Hungry astronaut
Drives off from the Cape to eat
In own lunching pad.

Sewer employee
Works underground, cheerfully
Sings: As Slime Goes By.

Tourist complaining:
Egypt me out of a tour
Of the pyramids.

Tater Tots, Yukon Gold,
Red Bliss, and Bill O'Reilly,
The Common Tater.

Osculating with
Great passion, the lovers press
To make their lipstick.

Entomologist:
My own maggotism will
Attract the ladies.

**Proliferation
Of porn films continues by
Popular dement.**

Constructing a home
With numerous windows can
Be very paneful.

No matter how much
You push the envelope, it's
Still stationery.

Poker champ decides
To teach his style, which he calls
Cardiology.

That ugly, smelly
Broad, he started to complain,
Wasn't worth a scent.

Convention speaker
Scratches groin, tells jokes – a case
Of jocular itch?

Teacher instructs class:
Your daily use of pencils
Make your work pointless.

Bill Clinton was the
Only prez able to score
Between two Bushes.

Paparazzi hound
Celebrities day and night,
Claim freedom of leech.

Crash a huge party
On a huge yacht and you learn
More about the swells.

Some Chinese gamblers
Have been taking their chances
By going Tibet.

**Tired Rumanian
Goes to travel agency
Just to Bucharest.**

**Army medics search
Broadway for new theatre
Of operations.**

Hate jalapeños,
Dislike cuchifritos, and
Chili leaves me cold.

Florist on cycle
Selling bouquets of roses
Is petal pusher.

Man professes total
Failure as a new golfer,
No ifs, and or putts.

Old gent takes his young
Bride for a great honeymoon
At Viagra Falls.

Man with restless leg
Syndrome tries best ways for a
Feetal position.

Borrowing can lead
You into the valley of
The shadow of debt.

Serb couple have a
Fight at Yule, she missile toes
Him in the Balkans.

Headless Horseman is Character in the Legend Of Creepy Hollow.

Seventeen Seventy-Six,
Rebel cooks would either shoot
Or cacciatore.

Homesick lizard in
The zoo hissing out: "Gee. Mom,
Iguana go home."

**Coffee maven dies,
Medical examiner
Decoffinates him.**

Dairy farmer says
Some cheeses are quite good but
Others are gouda.

**Celebration of
Son's bar-mitzvah was filled with
Much Jewbilation.**

Inexperienced
Boxer warned by trainer not
To play with matches.

**Cannibal eats a
Missionary, gets a good
Taste of religion.**

Mathematician,
His circumference quite wide
From life full of pi.

Drug rehab center
Sign posted on the front lawn
Reads, "Keep Off the Grass."

Rather than joining
Dangerous cults, you really
Should practice safe sects.

Congregants' chatter
Prevents the thoughtful cleric
From consecrating.

Congress between two
Representatives might well
Raise a few eyebrows.

**Some dairy products
Hailed for originating
Orgasmically.**

Shot crook crumbles, falls
Onto the hard ground in a
Fatal position.

British dentist sued:
Patient claims that his London
Bridge is falling down.

Father of wrestler
Praises his offspring as the
Grapple of his eye.

I've seen men farming
I've seen kids farming,
Never fish farming.

Huge grizzly credits
Strength to grandpas and grandmas,
His revered fourbears.

Horse ranch, sheep wander
In, cowboy warns shepherd: "Get
The flock out of here."

Dinner time, a Greek
Housewife prepares a salad
Light as a feta.

New Orleans native
To friend: "Family OK?"
"Yes, and how's bayou?"

Russet potato
And Idaho potato
Spend night in the sack.

Forgets to prepare
For tomorrow's dinner guests,
Checks his collender.

"Not even a kiss
On the cheek," she warned, "for I
Am impeckable."

Saxophonist mounts
Stage, walks toward his chair, trips,
Falls down on his brass.

Beer drinking couples
Woozily promise their love
On Ballentine's Day.

Slovakian chess
Master drives westward and tries
To find a Czech mate.

Superstitious gent
Always seems reluctant to
Read his horrorscope.

Criminal cases
Require defense attorneys
And persecutors.

**Count Dracula: "A
Merry Christmas to all and
To all a good fright."**

Hooker claims that each
Night she turned tricks she was cool,
Calm and collected.

Many products on
Store shelves are clumsily boxed
And manufractured.

Pillsbury Doughboy
Suddenly dies, grave site is
Soon piled high with flours.

The Wall Street bailout:
Dermatologists warned Street:
Don't devise rash moves.

Egregious lack of
Fish in pond, the egret
Egressed with regret.

He cared not for all
Her meat dishes, but found last
Night's to be the wurst.

Crampy guest speaker
Starts talk, becomes stricken, gets
 Vowels in uproar.

She to a suitor:
"If I knew you were coming
I'd have baked a snake."

Smart farmer tries to
Introduce his proper goose
With propaganda.

The law confiscates
A pimp's luxury auto –
Cadillac arrest?

Lepidopterist
Visits army mess hall to
Watch the butter fly.

Geneticist sings
His favorite popular
Tune: "Send in the Clones."

Honeymooners fly:
Oahu today, and the
Next isle to Maui.

Foreign diplomat
Arrested for spying – this
An attaché case?

Girl friend of Mickey
Mouse suffers what doctor says
Is a Minnie stroke.

At organ donor
Facility restroom, sign reads:
Wash glands thoroughly.

Congressman tames his
Horse with non-stop talk; call him
A filly buster.

Computer addict
Convinced she can cover her
Mattress with spread sheets.

Two golfers argue
Harshly over their scores. This
Is pair for the coarse!

"I bet you can get
Her to roll between sheets." "I'm
Not a bedding man."

Spices good for your
Spirit and great for basil
Metabolic rate.

State Senate: "We need
A new reservoir." The Gov:
"I don't give a damn."

His mother-in-law
Just arrived and he welcomed
Her with open qualms.

**Radio City
Music Hall, Christmas time – see
The Rockettes' red glare.**

If you want to find
Spiderman, just keep searching
For him on the web.

Proctologist hurt
Most of his patients; in fact,
He almost rectum.

Of all the great girls
In London, shmoe makes a move
To Picadilly.

Drama critic says
That new all female play is
Overly misscast.

Sickly physicist,
Filled with arthritis, complains
Of his mega hurts.

Backs into airplane
Propeller, a stupid stunt
For her *

Clumsy golf player
Endangers others with his
Beginner's fore!play.

Condemned convicts write
Down their biographies for
The jail noosepaper.